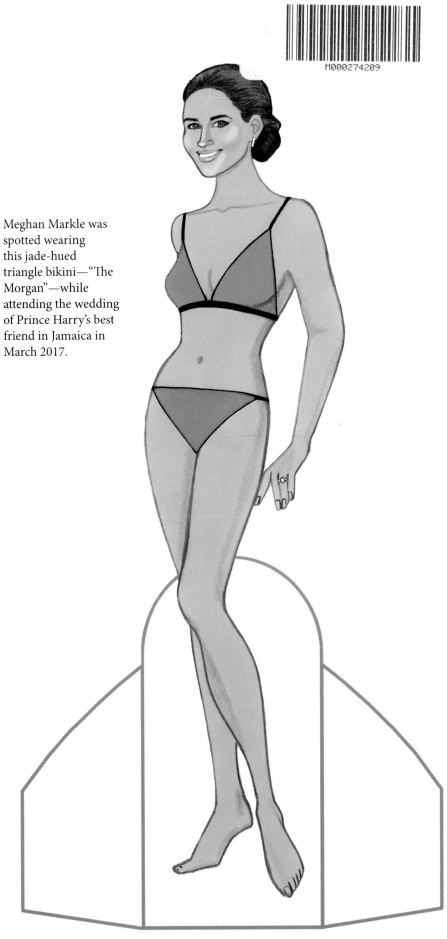

Meghan Markle was spotted wearing this jade-hued triangle bikini—"The Morgan"—while attending the wedding of Prince Harry's best friend in Jamaica in March 2017.

Meghan Markle

PLATE 1

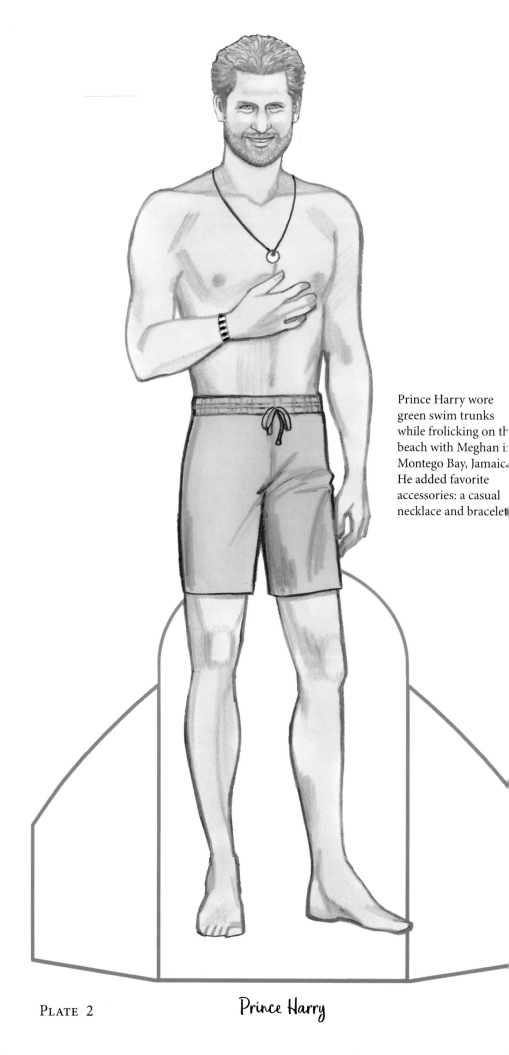

Prince Harry wore green swim trunks while frolicking on the beach with Meghan in Montego Bay, Jamaica. He added favorite accessories: a casual necklace and bracelet.

PLATE 2

Prince Harry

Do not cut out
the space between
Meghan's feet.

Meghan was definitely on-trend at the Invictus Games in Toronto in September 2017. She dressed in Mother Denim "Looker Fray" jeans and an oversized Misha Nonoo "husband" shirt, accessorized with tortoiseshell sunglasses, Sarah Flint "Natalie" ballet flats, and an Everlane Day Market tote.

PLATE 3

Prince Harry wore a polo t-shirt with the Invictus Games logo, belted casual pants, and athletic shoes to the event, adding a favorite bracelet on his right wrist.

Plate 4

The official announcement of the engagement of Prince Harry to Meghan Markle took place on November 27, 2017. Meghan wore the "Mara" wrap coat from LINE—the sold-out coat was renamed the "Meghan"—and "Matilde" pumps from Aquazzura.

PLATE 5

Dressed in a blue suit, white shirt, and black tie and shoes, Prince Harry appeared cool and calm as he and Meghan announced their engagement. A casual bracelet can be spotted on Prince Harry's right wrist.

PLATE 6

For the couple's November 27, 2017, engagement interview with the BBC, Meghan wore a sleeveless P.A.R.O.S.H. dress with an asymmetrical bow. Like the "Mara" wrap coat, the dress was renamed "The Meghan." The dress appears on Plate 5, under the LINE wrap coat.

PLATE 7

For the couple's first official event, on December 1, 2017—the World AIDS Day Charity Fair in Nottingham—Meghan wore the double-breasted "Elodie" coat from Mackage and carried a Strathberry tote.

PLATE 8

In Nottingham, Meghan selected the Joseph "Laurel" skirt, worn with Kurt Geiger "Violet" boots, and a Wolford top. Plate 8 shows the Joseph skirt worn with the Mackage "Elodie" coat.

PLATE 9

The prince dressed casually in a blue blazer, open-necked white shirt, black pants, and blue suede lace-up shoes for the visit to Nottingham Academy.

PLATE 10

Meghan and Prince Harry posed for their official engagement photo on December 21, 2017. Meghan chose a Ralph & Russo black tulle gown with hand-appliquéd gold threadwork—it caused a stir because of its sheer fabric.

PLATE 11

Meghan attended a pre-Christmas luncheon hosted by the Queen at Buckingham Palace wearing a Nightshade midi dress from the Self-Portrait label and Birks Snowflake® earrings.

PLATE 12

For Christmas with the royals at Sandringham, Meghan chose a Sentaler alpaca coat, Philip Treacy hat, Stuart Weitzman "Highland" boots, and Chloe "Pixie" handbag.

PLATE 13

This Club Monaco "Tay
wrap dress, tied in a bo
at the waist, was one of
Meghan's choices for
Christmas with the roy
family at Sandringham.

PLATE 14

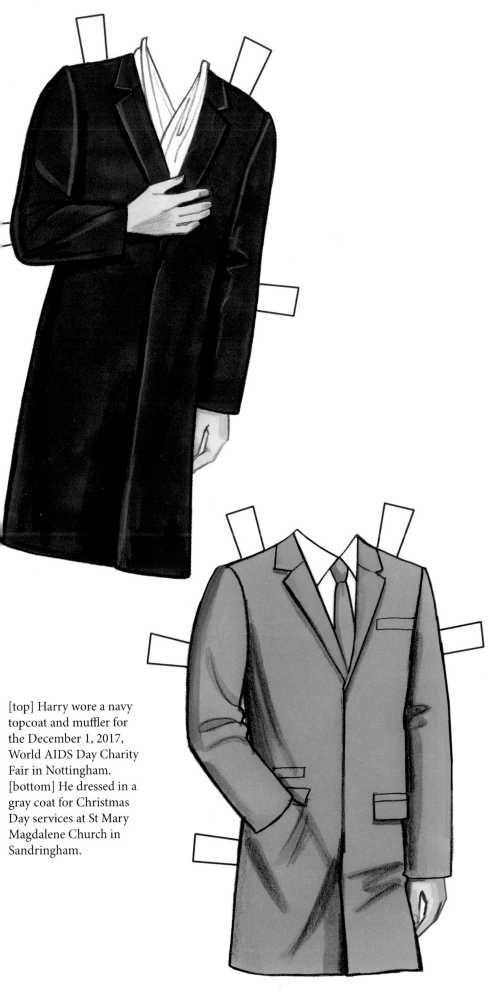

[top] Harry wore a navy topcoat and muffler for the December 1, 2017, World AIDS Day Charity Fair in Nottingham. [bottom] He dressed in a gray coat for Christmas Day services at St Mary Magdalene Church in Sandringham.

PLATE 15

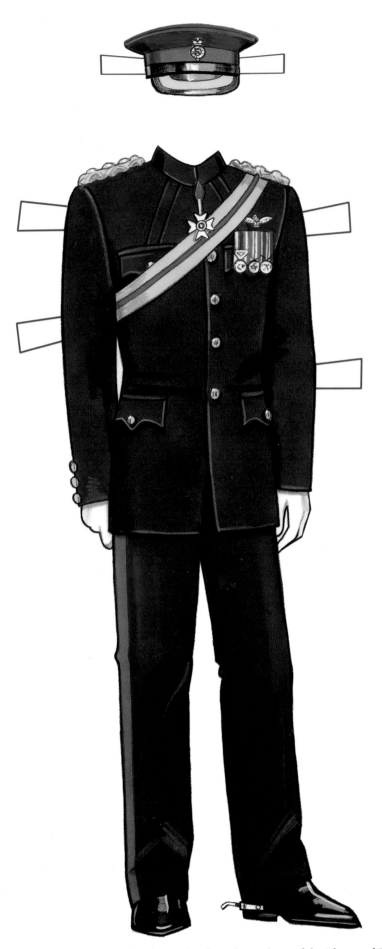

Prince Harry is resplendent in his "number 1 dress of the Blues and Royals" uniform (representing the cavalry regiment of the British Army).

PLATE 16